SPIRIT OF
BRITISH TRAMS
A CONCISE HISTORY

ROBIN JONES

First published in Great Britain in 2011
Copyright text © 2011 Robin Jones.

British Library Cataloguing-in-Publication Data
A CIP record for this title is available from the British Library

ISBN 978 0 85710 048 1

PiXZ Books
Halsgrove House, Ryelands Business Park,
Bagley Road, Wellington, Somerset TA21 9PZ
Tel: 01823 653777, Fax: 01823 216796
email: sales@halsgrove.com

An imprint of Halstar Ltd, part of the
Halsgrove group of companies
Information on all Halsgrove titles is
available at: www.halsgrove.com

Printed and bound in China by
Topan Leefung Printing Ltd

To Alma, who rode on the 'boneshakers' of Coventry

Snaefell Mountain Railway tram No 5, seen high above the cloud line at the Summit Station.

It may seem an obvious question to ask, but what exactly do we mean by 'tram'?

A tramway is another word for railway, and more specifically today, a railway used by bus-like vehicles that runs through streets as opposed to a separate trackbed of its own. Many early railways that pre-dated the steam age, relying on horses, gravity or even manpower for traction were referred to as 'tramways'. Similarly operations, such as the Volks Electric Railway at Brighton or the Manx Electric Railway, have more in common with the commonly-accepted notion of what comprises a tramway.

The distinction is again blurred when you look at conventional railways that run through streets, like the Great Western Railway's Weymouth Quay branch, used by main line trains running through the heart of the town to meet cross-Channel ferries, or the Glyn Valley Tramway in central Wales, which had conventional steam locomotives with their wheels 'boxed in' to protect fellow road users from being caught up in them, but was far more akin to a conventional railway.

Fans of Thomas the Tank Engine will be familiar with Toby the Tram Engine, a type of motive power looking like a sort of railway brakevan but which can move under its own power and was fitted with cowcatchers. It was based on prototypes which famously ran on the Wisbech & Upwell Tramway in East Anglia and the harbour lines at Ipswich and Great Yarmouth, all of which fall firmly into the 'railway' category.

The world's first passenger-carrying railway was originally known as the Oystermouth Railway or Tramroad Company, but better known by its later name of the Swansea & Mumbles Railway. It opened in 1806 to carry minerals between Swansea and Oystermouth (Mumbles), and which a year later obtained permission to carry passengers, beginning services on 25 March.

Some say this was also Britain's first tramway, as the horse-drawn passenger vehicles bore a remarkable similarity to

Swansea Museum has a nearby Tramway Centre which includes this replica of the original horse-drawn Mumbles tram which ran between the city and Oystermouth, and a complete replica of a later town centre tram.

stagecoaches, although they ran on rails, but it did not share any of its route with street traffic until a turnpike road was built alongside it in the 1820s. The tramway term would most certainly have been applicable then.

The words tram and tramway were sixteenth-century Scottish terms for the wagons and tracks used inside coal mines. In turn they may have originated from a North Sea Germanic word referring to the beam or shaft of a barrow or sledge, or the barrow itself. In the USA, what we would call street trams were from around 1840 referred to as 'streetcars' or 'horsecars', pulled by horses or mules. When tramlines were electrified, they became trolleycars or simply trolleys, a term which may have originated from the troller, a four-wheel device that was dragged along dual overhead wires by a cable linking it to the roof of the vehicle. Britain imported this term only in references to the successor to many street tramways, the trolleybus, a hybrid between a motor bus, running on pneumatic tyres without rail guidance, and that part of a tram which relied on electrical pickup from overhead wires.

The Isle of Man's 3ft gauge 1.6-mile seafront promenade Douglas Bay Horse Tramway is a rare survivor from the days when such operations were commonplace, especially in London. It was built and initially operated by retired Sheffield civil engineer Thomas Lightfoot and apart from World War Two has run every year.

The world's first streetcar line was the New York and Harlem Railroad's Fourth Avenue Line which ran along the Bowery and Fourth Avenue in New York, and which began operating in 1832. Three years later, a similar line began operating in New Orleans; it now claims to be the world's oldest continuously-operating street railway system.

An attempt to launch London's first street tramway came as early as 1857, copying these US models. Four years after the first tramway in Paris was authorised, the London General Omnibus Company issued a prospectus for the London Omnibus Tramway Co. Ltd, with a proposal for a double-track line running in the centre of the road from Notting Hill Gate through Bayswater and along the New Road, City Road and Moorgate to Bank, with a branch from King's Cross via Farringdon Street to Fleet Street.

The omnibuses to run on the tracks would be hauled by two horses and each carried 60 passengers, three times the number of the existing road vehicles.

The idea went down like a lead balloon. Sir Benjamin Hall, MP for Marylebone and Chief Commissioner of Public Works, complained that his carriage had been overturned on plateway railways in South Wales, and the enabling bill was defeated in Parliament at its second reading.

Britain's first tramway appeared on Liverpool's dockside in March 1859, its originator, Englishman William Joseph Curtis, having inspected the Paris line four years earlier. It ran until January 1860.

However, it was an American, George Francis Train, who opened Britain's first true permanent street tramway, in Birkenhead on 30 August 1860.

Train, one of the most famous people in the world in his day, was a businessman, politician, author, lecturer and globetrotter who provided inspiration for Jules Verne's *Around the World in Eighty Days*, and all-around larger-than-life character. His surname was perfect for someone who had helped set up the Union Pacific Railroad.

George Francis Train, who founded Britain's first successful permanent street tramway in Birkenhead.

Train then sought permission to open lines in London's streets, and was allowed to lay one along Bayswater Road between Marble Arch and Porchester Terrace, opening on 23 March 1861, a second from Westminster Abbey down Victoria Street which started running on 15 April that year and a third from Westminster Bridge to Kennington Gate, which opened on 15 August.

Mass complaints about the fact that the rails protruded above road surfaces and caused obstructions led to these lines being removed after only a few months. Train, who was even arrested and fined because of the problems, also had not seen that affluent areas where horse buses had been refused permission to ply their trade would object to incursions by tram lines, while middle and working class people would welcome the cheap transport that they could provide.

The tramway cause received a major boost in December 1868 when supporter John Bright became President of the Board of Trade.

Two of the last London trams in service pass on Westminster Bridge on July 21 1951, nine months before this type of transport became extinct in London.

The following year, Bills to build 'experimental' tramways south of the Thames were presented by the Metropolitan Street Tramways and the Pimlico, Peckham & Greenwich Street Tramways, while the North Metropolitan Tramways, looked to east London. All three of them were authorised, with the North Metropolitan ordered its first tramcars to be built by the New

York firm of John Stephenson & Company, which picked up many orders as demand exceeded supply.

Metropolitan Street Tramways trams, seating 22 passengers inside and 24 outside, began running along Brixton Road from Brixton to Kennington Church on 2 May 1870, the route being completed to its northern terminus at Westminster Bridge Road on 5 October, and to Clapham Road on 7 December.

The North Metropolitan carried more than a million passengers on its Bow-Whitechapel route during its first six months after opening on 9 May 1870.

A star exhibit at the London Transport Museum in Covent Garden is London Tramways Company double deck horse tram No 284, built by John Stephenson & Co in New York in 1882. These tramcars were built to a similar design to horse buses, but had a platform and staircase at both ends. At the end of the line, the horses were unhitched, led round and attached to the other end of the tram for the return journey. The tramcar itself did not have to be turned around.

The new tram companies all adopted the standard gauge, with the aim of linking up their services at later dates. A typical tramcar was pulled by two horses and while they carried 60 passengers, they were cheaper, roomier, and safer than the horse buses and hackney carriages and offered a much smoother ride. It was far easier for two horses to pull a heavy vehicle running on smooth iron rails than on an uneven road service.

All three companies charged no more than a penny a mile, subject to a minimum fare of threepence. They were also obliged to offer workmen's fares at a halfpenny per mile.

The Tramways Act 1870 was a key step in the development of urban transport in Britain. Following the experiences with Train in London, the Act aimed to promote tramways by clarifying and regulating the legal position.

It gave local councils the power to grant a 21-year concession to a private tramway operator. The operator could construct the track as part of the concession but was responsible for the repair of the public highway between the tracks and a short distance either side. At the conclusion of the lease, the local authority could purchase the complete undertaking, including the trams and horses.

However, despite fierce and prolonged Parliamentary battles during 1870-2, none of the three London tram operators were allowed into the heart of the city, largely due to objections from property owners. Instead, the companies concentrated on developing their systems in the suburbs.

By 1875, the London companies had 350 tram cars between them and nearly 55 miles of lines, but already moves were underway to replace horses with self-propelled traction, as happened on the railways decades before.

Just as steam locomotives replaced horse traction on early railways, it was a logical step forward to looking at the possibility of self-propelled street trams superseding horse trams.

However, while omnibus operators were still making big profits from running horse buses, there was little incentive to replace them with a better form of transport: indeed, the early steam carriage experiments had not been anywhere near as successful as the introduction of steam locomotives on railways, and so road transport was lagging behind in several fields.

Two steam buses carried passengers in Edinburgh in the early 1870s, but running such vehicles on rails rather than roads was seen to offer much better physical support.

London civil engineer John Grantham demonstrated an experimental 23ft steam-powered double-ended four-wheel open-top tramcar at a railway arch in Salamanca Street, Lambeth in March 1873.

The mechanism had been constructed by Merryweather & Sons of Greenwich, a firm which built steam fire engines, and the body by Oldbury Railway Carriage & Wagon Works. It could hold 60 passengers, having seats for 20 inside and 24 on top.

Grantham died in July 1874, and after the machine was successfully demonstrated to the Council of the Society of Arts, he was posthumously awarded the Howard Medal, a prize offered to anyone inventing a locomotive to replace horse traction on trams.

His vehicle entered service on the Wantage Tramway in Oxfordshire on 1 August 1876, becoming Britain's first public steam tram, and lasted in service for 23 years.

Dick Kerr-built steam tram No 18 of the North London Tramways Co, hauling an 1885 Falcon bogie trailer car.

The steam tram was adopted by several cities both in the West Midlands and north of England and on the continent during the 1870s and '80s, but legislation passed in 1879 limited their speed to 10mph, barred the emission of smoke or steam, and decreed that working parts of the engine, including the wheels, were to be screened from public view.

Huddersfield Corporation opened its first steam tram route on 11 January 1883, making it Britain's first municipally-operated tramway, as opposed to a private system.

One big problem with steam trams was the fact that the lightly-laid horse tram tracks in the streets could not carry their weight.

Croydon became a centre of experimentation with new forms of tram traction, the Croydon Tramways Company running mechanical trams to run over its lines.

In 1891 a Mr Jarman carried out trials along the London Road

Above left: Stored inside London Transport Museum's Acton depot, Class E/1 electric tram No 1025 of 1910 (left) stands alongside Type UCC Feltham electric tram No 355 of 1931. The Felthams were the most modern of all London double deck trams.

Above right: West Ham Corporation Tramways double deck electric tram No 102, which dates from 1910, inside London Transport Museum.

line to Thornton Heath using Croydon double-deck four-wheeled horse tramcars converted to electric traction, the body having been remounted on a stronger underframe to take the extra weight and to allow room for the electrical apparatus and traction motor mounted beneath.

The accumulator system saw accumulators or a basic rechargeable battery stored under the seats on the car and they were recharged at the tram depot.

Jarman's Electric Car entered service in December 1891.

The Electric Tramcar Syndicate Limited produced a tramcar worked by battery-electric propulsion which entered service on London Road in January 1894, but was withdrawn two months later due to fumes from the sulphuric battery acid spreading upwards into the passenger compartment.

The syndicate, which later became British Electrical Street Tramways Ltd., also experimented with a gas-powered tram at Croydon in 1893. The Croydon and the London, Deptford & Greenwich Tramways systems also tried out an oil-powered tram in the 1890s. And Londoner Andrew Smith Hallidie, who had introduced cable cars to San Francisco in the early 1870s, opened a London version between Archway Tavern and Highgate in 1889. It was closed in 1892, reopened in 1897

Cable tram 'dummy' No 6 and trailer at Highgate Hill, on an Archway Tavern to Highgate service in 1884.

and lasted in that form until 1909. London Tramways opened a cable line between Kennington and Brixton in the 1890s, and it lasted until 1894.

However, it was electric traction that won the day.

In 1837, Scotsman Robert Davidson demonstrated an early battery-electric locomotive on the Edinburgh & Glasgow Railway, but this method was not considered a realistic alternative until 1866, when a vastly-improved type of dynamo became available, devised by German scientist and engineer Werner von Siemens, who later joined forces with mechanical engineer, Johann Georg Halske. They ran a model electric railway at the Berlin Trade Fair in 1879, and in 1881 launched trial services at Lichterfelde, on what became the world's first electric railway/tramway. Thomas Alva Edison also experimented with electric traction in New York in the early 1880s.

It was Magnus Volk who brought the concept to Britain, and switched the country on.

The son of a German clockmaker, Magnus Volk was born at 35 (now 40) Western Road, Brighton on 19 October 1851. Locally educated, he became apprenticed to a scientific instrument maker but his true passion lay in the worlds of science and engineering, in particular electricity.

In 1879, he successfully demonstrated the first telephone link in Brighton. The next year, he connected the first residential fire alarm to the fire station and became the first resident of

Left: *Magnus Volk.*

Below: *Volks' Electric Railway was both the first electric railway and electric tramway in Britain, and is still giving sterling service along Brighton's eastern sea front.*

Brighton to fit electric lights to his house at 38 Dyke Road.

On 4 August 1883, Volk unveiled a quarter-mile-long 2ft gauge electric railway running from a site on the seashore opposite the town's aquarium to the Chain Pier. Power was provided by a 2hp Otto gas engine driving a Siemens D5 50 volt DC generator. A small electric car was fitted with a 1½hp motor giving a top speed of about 6mph. Yet from these humble 'seafront novelty' beginnings, it was the precursor not only of our electric tramways, but also the London Underground lines and the parts of the national rail network that were later electrified, such as the East and West Coast main lines.

The idea of an electric as opposed to steam locomotive may have originated in Scotland, but Volk brought it back to Britain in the form of a workable concept.

Volk extended his line eastwards, widened the track to 2ft 9in gauge and designed two more powerful and bigger passenger cars, reopening on 4 April 1884.

Volk's railway is still with us today, albeit on a slightly shorter route, and is of immense historical importance as the world's oldest electric line still running.

The second British electric line was the Giant's Causeway, Portrush & Bush Valley Tramway opened in 1883, at first worked by steam, and was followed by the Bessbrook & Newry Tramway in 1885.

A Giant's Causeway, Portrush & Bush Valley Tramway passing the ruins of Dunluce Castle in 1890.

On 29 September 1885, the legendary Blackpool Tramway was opened. Built to 4ft 8½in, the railway network's standard gauge, the first section ran for nearly three miles, mainly along the seafront, from Cocker Street to Dean Street, the work of Halifax engineer Michael Holroyd Smith. Then came the Ryde Pier Tramway on the Isle of Wight, a horse tram line of 1864 electrified in March 1886, and the short-lived Gravesend & Northfleet Tramway, which ran from 1889-90 using an innovative but unsuccessful system whereby the power supply was picked up from beneath one of the running rails.

A successful demonstration of a tramway picking up power from overhead cables was given at the International Exhibition in Edinburgh between June and November 1890.

Following this, the Roundhay Park Tramway in Leeds opened in October 1891, using overhead power, which became the predominant though not only means of powering tramways in Britain. Blackpool, which had initially used a power pick-up between the running rails, converted to overhead pick-up in 1899.

The Bristol Tramways & Carriage Company opened its first electrified tramline from Bristol to Kingswood in October in 1895.

London County Council decided to buy up all the tramways under its jurisdiction, and lease the lines to private operators. It began operating its own horse tram services on 24 miles of routes in south London bought on 1 January 1899 from the London Tramways Company.

Full-scale electrification began with Imperial Tramways which took over the rundown tram network in West London and extended it from Shepherds Bush to Acton, Ealing, Chiswick and Uxbridge, under the banner of the London United Tramways Company, using overhead electrification throughout and its own network of power stations. Launching public services on 4 April 1901, it was the first of its kind in the London area. Two months later, East Ham Corporation began running its own electric trams, followed in September in Croydon run by the British Electric Traction Company Ltd, and the Metropolitan Electric Tramways lines in Middlesex and Hertfordshire.

Overhead wires were cheap to install and maintain, gave the most effective use of current and were the most reliable form of power, but were deemed unsightly, and so when London County Council embarked in its own electrification scheme in late 1901, it chose a more expensive conduit system with conductor rails placed beneath the surface of the roadway.

The first section of the council's routes to be electrified was that between the southern side of Westminster and Blackfriar

A fleet of electric London trams and the horse trams they were superseding, pictured at Kennington Park Road. The electric tram, C class open-top car No 91 is on the first electrified route, which opened in May 1903, while the horse tram is on the Kennington-Streatham service, which closed for electrification in April 1904.

Left: *Decorated Class A tram No 86 is pictured on its return journey from Kennington to Westminster following the opening of the first section of London County Council's electric tramway by the Prince of Wales (later King George V) on 15 May 1903. He can be seen standing on the top deck of the tram at front.*

Bridges, and Tooting, on 15 May 1903. Highly successful, it paved the way for rapid electrification and the construction of route extensions and new lines.

By 1910, the county council had electrified nearly 120 route miles, running beyond the city boundary in many places.

The Kingsway Tramway Subway became the only underground tramway route in London, opening in February 1906 and linking the tramway systems north and south of the Thames via the Embankment.

The Edwardian era saw a mass explosion in the building and electrifying of tram routes in towns and cities throughout Britain, and by 1910, there were more than 300 tramways, nearly half of them opened in the first decade of the twentieth century.

By 1914, the combined London area tram operators including municipal operators in outlying boroughs comprised the largest tram network in Europe. However, the outbreak of the First World War called a halt to the expansion of tramways, as tens of thousands of drivers, conductors and other staff joined the armed forces to be replaced by 'stand-in' female staff. The final London horse tram was withdrawn during World War One.

The writing on the wall for trams had by then begun to appear, with only five new lines opening during 1910-13. The motor omnibus had begun to appear and offered far greater flexibility, especially in places where tram routes had been found to be unprofitable. Britain's first tramway abandonment was that of the Sheerness & District Electric Power & Traction Company in 1917, its services being replaces by buses. Also, on 20 June 1911, Britain's first trolleybus routes were opened in Leeds and Bradford, and nine more appeared before 1920, although at first they did not replace existing tramlines.

Only three tramways were electrified in the 1920s, the aforementioned Swansea & Mumbles Railway, Edinburgh Corporation Tramways which had hitherto used cable haulage and the Dearne & District Light Railways. Passenger levels on

UK tramways reached an all-time high in 1927/8, with more than 4,700 million journeys made. Stiff competition from rival forms of street transport including vast improvements made in motorbus and coach and trolleybus technology afterwards saw the rot gradually set in.

On 21 November 1922, the first conversion of a tramline to a trolleybus route in Britain place between Birmingham city centre and the inner-city suburbs of Nechells.

The 1930s marked the start of a mass abandonment of tramways. As road traffic increased, a Royal Commission on Transport in 1930 said that because trams could not be steered, they were more likely to be involved in collisions than other vehicles, and were causing obstructions to other vehicles. It was recommended that no more tramways should be built and the existing ones phased out. The motorbus, not the trolleybus, was considered as ultimately the best way forward.

Luftwaffe air raids during World War Two helped several tram systems on their way to closure. Coventry's trams never ran again after the raid on 14/15 November and a direct hit on the Bristol system's power supply on 11 April 1941 saw it close for good too. On the other hand, austerity measures that would have led to their replacement by buses gave other tramlines around the country a breathing space of a few years, and some cities, like Leeds, even extended lines after the war, while others, including Blackpool, Sheffield, Edinburgh, Glasgow and Aberdeen, ordered new tramcars.

However, the first postwar abandonment was that of Hull Corporation's lines in June 1945. The 1950s hastened the closure of both tram and trolleybus routes, and London's trams ceased operation after 5 July 1952. Birmingham closed its tramways the following year.

The last closure was that of the Glasgow routes on 2 September 1962, leaving only Blackpool with trams. Even so, Blackpool implemented route closures, leaving just the lines along the sea front and to Fleetwood we delight in today.

In 1951, a group of volunteers led by transport historian Tom Rolt took over the all-but-defunct Talyllyn Railway in central Wales and kickstarted the operational heritage railway movement which today has more than 100 lines and is a major contributor to the UK tourist economy. Rolt also heavily campaigned to save the country's canals from closure.

Around this time, trams too became the target of preservationists, but on a far smaller scale than their railway counterparts.

The last tram to run in London was to Abbey Wood on 5 July 1952, the event being preceded by Last Tram Week, with banners draped over the remaining vehicles and special tickets issued to passengers. The final operational tram, car No 1951 arrived at south-east London's New Cross depot early the following morning, driven by John Cliff, deputy chairman of London Transport Executive, who had started his career as a tram driver. At New Cross depot the packed tram was greeted by LTE chairman Lord Latham, who proclaimed: "In the name of Londoners I say goodbye, old tram."

A band of enthusiasts on a farewell tour of Southampton Tramways in August 1948 bought open top tramcar No 45, on which they had just ridden, for £10, and hit upon the idea of a museum of working trams. The group developed into the Tramway Museum Society which was founded in 1955.

Trams in High Street, Southampton, in an early twentieth century view.

The society looked for a suitable site and in 1959 came across derelict Cliff Quarry at Crich in Derbyshire, which had been worked by none other than George Stephenson, the 'father of the railways', and who had built the world's first metre gauge railway to carry limestone from the quarry to his limekilns at Ambergate alongside the North Midland Railway. Talyllyn volunteers were already recovering track components from the line for their own scheme.

The society agreed to lease part of the site and buildings, and later bought it, transforming it into the National Tramway Museum, with working tram lines powered by overhead wires and street scenes typical of urban tram routes, relocating buildings from elsewhere and installing typical street furniture. Now known as Crich Tramway Village, it has Britain's finest collection of street trams and is considered to be one of the country's top museums.

Another organisation looking for someone to run preserved street trams in 1959 was the Leeds University Union Railway

Society which had saved Leeds tramcars. Under the auspices of lecturer the late Dr Fred Youell, its student members took over the city's redundant Middleton Railway, which had run continuously since 1858 and had just been closed.

However, while several trams were moved there at first, the venture did not take off as a tram venue, but as one of the first two standard gauge preserved railways in Britain, the other being the Bluebell Railway in Sussex.

The first heritage era train that ran during 20-24 June 1960, the inaugural week of volunteer-run services, was not hauled by steam, but Hunslet 0-6-0 diesel No 1697 pulling none other than the only complete Swansea & Mumbles Railway tramcar to be saved. Very sadly, the condition of this tramcar, No 2, deteriorated, and after it was declared unsafe to run and no other society was prepared to take it on, it was scrapped in 1969.

The unlikely marriage of trams and railways in preservation took another twist with the establishment of the 2ft 9in gauge Seaton Tramway along the trackbed of the Southern Region branch line to the East Devon resort, which closed on 7 March 1966.

In 1949, Claude Lane, owner of the Lancaster Electrical Company in Barnet, which made milk floats and other battery-electric vehicles, built a portable 15in gauge tram based on ex-Darwen Tramways Car 23, then running on the Llandudno & Colwyn Bay system. Hugely popular as an attraction at fêtes, Claude leased a permanent site at Eastbourne in 1953, and set up Modern Electric Tramways Ltd to operate a two-thirds-of-a-mile 2ft gauge line and built more scale-down replicas to run over it.

The growth of Eastbourne's road system began to squeeze the tramway out and while looking for a freehold site, he heard about the plans to close the Seaton branch and bought the Colyton-Seaton section from British Railways.

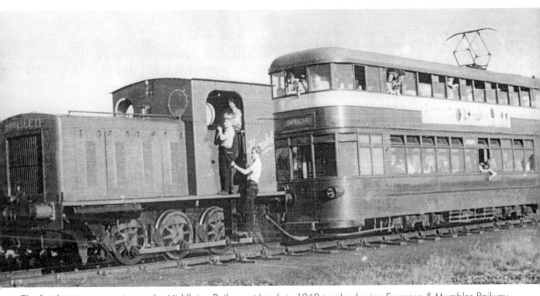

The first heritage era trains on the Middleton Railway at Leeds in 1960 involved using Swansea & Mumbles Railway Car 2 as a passenger coach.

On 28 August 1970, Car 8 became the first tram to run in passenger service on the new 2ft 9in gauge, taking power from a battery car as overhead wires had yet to be installed. Claude died from a heart attack on 2 April 1971. A new Seaton terminus was established in 1975, and the final extension to Colyton completed in 1980, making a total of three miles.

Several of the trams in use on the line are genuine trams from the last century, but they have been dismantled and cut down to size, to make them about two thirds as big as the originals, making the Seaton Tramway unique in this respect. The line has also built several new trams, and today carries around 100,000 passengers a year.

The Manchester Transport Museum Society was founded in 1961 with the aim of creating a museum, and chose Heaton Park, into which a Manchester Corporation Tramways line had been extended on 31 May 1903, running until it was replaced by buses and a tarmacadamed road in 1934.

The society decided to reopen the old tramway spur from Middleton Road to the old tram shelter some 300 yards inside the park, lifting the tarmacadam covering the original track. The Heaton Park Tramway was officially opened on the 28 March 1980, and was later extended to a new terminus near the boating lake.

Its operating fleet includes electric trams and unique Eades patent reversible horse tram L53, which ran on the Manchester Carriage and Tramways Company lines.

In 1965, the East Anglia Transport Museum was set up in a meadow near Carlton Colville outside Lowestoft, following the rescue of the body of Lowestoft tram No 14 which had been turned into a summerhouse. It houses a wealth of historic vehicles, many of them restored, and the excellent museum not only has a tramway but a trolleybus circuit too, as well as the short 2ft gauge East Suffolk Light Railway. The trams and trolleybuses began offering rides in 1981 following the construction of a roadway, and is the only museum in the country where visitors can ride on both as well as trains and buses.

Beamish, The North of England Open Air Museum in Country Durham, which opened in 1972 and which has superbly showcased examples of everyday life in urban and rural north east England in the early twentieth century, as well as becoming a world leader in research into early railways, has a one-and-a-half-mile electric tram circuit which links all the individual townscapes and industrial heritage attractions and offering breathtaking views over the surrounding countryside. The similar and equally excellent Black Country Living Museum in Dudley also has an electric tram line on which restored local vehicles are used to give visitors rides.

Glasgow's tramways were built to the unusual gauge of 4 feet 7¾ inches to allow 4ft 8½in standard gauge railway wagons to be operated over parts of the system using their wheel flanges running in the slots of the tram tracks to access some shipyards. The first electric route began operations on 13 October 1898 and horse tram services ended in April 1902. The city's first purpose-built electric trams were 20 single deck vehicles with a central entrance. They lasted eight years in service. One was converted to a mains testing car and is now preserved in its original condition and No 672 in Glasgow Museum of Transport. Behind it is postwar Cunarder double decker No 1192, one of the last double-decker types to be built in the UK.

On 14 April 1995, tram history turned full circle when a 'new' street tramway using Hong Kong-built 1948-style vehicles was opened in Birkenhead, where Train had successfully launched his landmark operation in 1860. The Wirral Tramway runs from Wirral Transport Museum a mile to the Mersey Ferry service at Woodside.

The museum tramway collection was set up in collaboration with volunteers from Merseyside Tramway Preservation Society.

Meanwhile, trams have made a major comeback in Britain's cities. Worsening road congestion following soaring levels of car ownership saw planners look again at the tram concept, and draw up several light rail schemes. The first to open was the Manchester Metrolink on 6 April 1992, followed by the Sheffield Supertram on 21 March 1994. The first line of the Midland Metro which has light rail vehicles running on the former Great Western Railway trackbed from revived Birmingham Snow Hill Station to Wolverhampton followed in June 1999, the same month as the first tram ran on the new Croydon Tramlink, the first section of which was officially opened on 10 May 2000.

Nottingham and Edinburgh have also invested in modern light rail tram systems while schemes have been proposed for Belfast, Portsmouth and Southampton and Liverpool amongst others.

Far from being an anachronism, such developments suggest that street trams may well have been ahead of their time.

Opposite: The first electric street tram bought by enthusiasts was Southampton Corporation Tramways No 45, which was built in 1903. It was sold for £10 in 1949.

Cardiff City Tramways Car 131 was the first tram to be brought by enthusiasts to Crich in 1959, and it took half a century to restore to operational condition. It is not a converted passenger vehicle but a purpose-built works car for the purpose of watering the tracks. Constructed by Brush in 1905, it was the last survivor of the Cardiff tramways, and is seen running at Beamish during an April 2010 visit.

A recreated early twentieth-century urban street scene at Crich Tramway Village sees London Passenger Transport Board E1 car No 1622 (front) and Metropolitan Electric Tramways car No 331, one of five cars which entered service in London in December 1930 before being sold to Sunderland in 1937.

Tram driver and conductor at Crich Tramway Village.

Glasgow Corporation double decker No 1115 of 1929 and Leicester Car 76 of 1904 inside the exhibition hall at Crich.

Old soldier: unrestored Leamington & Warwick Tramways Car 1 was built in 1881 and is now exhibited inside Crich's exhibition hall.

Opposite: Leeds 399 dates from 1925 was the second passenger tram to arrive at Crich, although it was not restored until 1991.

Blackpool 1925-built balloon car No 712, where it now carries its original fleet number 249, stands at Crich alongside London Passenger Transport Board Car 1, constructed in 1932.

Opposite: *Liverpool Corporation Car 869 was built in 1936, sold to Glasgow in 1954, withdrawn six years later and is now at Crich.*

Top right: Blackpool tram No 633, built by Brush in 1937, was remodelled as a fishing trawler for the resort's illuminations.

Opposite: Preserved 1953-built Coronation car No 600 and newly-restored English Electric boat car No 600 with the famous tower in the background.

Bottom right: Blackpool English Electric double decker 'balloon cars' Nos 701 and 704, which date from 1934, pictured on the promenade in 1984. The 11-mile line is one of only a few operational tramways in the world which use double-deckers.

Blackpool open-top balloon car No 706, built by English Electric in 1934.

Opposite: Preserved Blackpool Standard tram No 147, built by Hurst Nelson in 1924.

Above left: *Beamish Museum-based 1950-built Sheffield 'Roberts' tram No 513 and 1903-built Stockport Car 5 at Blackpool Tramway's Rigby Road depot.*

Above right: *Liverpool Corporation Tramways Car No 762, normally based at the Heaton Park Tramway, taking part in the Blackpool Tramways 125th anniversary parade.*

Opposite: *Blackpool Tramways No 4, also known as No 31, and which dates from 1901, is part of the Beamish Museum fleet.*

Manchester 1914-built 'California' type tram No 765 running on the Heaton Park Tramway.

Opposite: *Manchester tram No 173, built in 1901 and in store at the city's Heaton Park Tramway.*

Above left: Gateshead single decker No 10 was built in 1926 and is now regularly running on the Beamish circuit.

Above right: Sheffield tram No 264, built in 1907, in service at Beamish Museum.

Opposite: The Heaton Park Tramway's award-winning restored Manchester Carriage and Tramways Company Eades patent reversible horse tram No L53, unique among surviving trams in that it uses the horses' own power to turn the body of the tram round on its underframe when reaching the end of the tracks. After being withdrawn it had been used as a hairdresser's and fish and chip shop in Glossop. It is seen on a visit to Beamish Museum.

Beamish Museum has been widely praised for recreating the past, and in November 2010, it had the chance to offer rides on Sunderland tram No 16 through a typical 'winter like they used to be'.

Opposite: *Yesterday once more: one of so many delightful scenes from the past recreated at Beamish Museum, this one featuring 1901-built Newcastle tram No 114.*

Ancient and modern side by side on the Wirral Tramway: Birkenhead Car 70 (left) was built in Hong Kong in 1992, while Liverpool No 762 was one of 12 bogie cars built in 1931/2 at Edge Lane Works. Withdrawn in 1955, the lower saloon became a bowling green clubhouse, but it was rescued by the Mersey Tramway Preservation Society in 1977, rebuilt and entered service on the Wirral Tramway in 2001.

Birkenhead Tramway Car 20 was built by the local firm of Milnes in 1900 and ran in the town for 37 years. After withdrawal, it stood on the banks of the River Dee, south of Chester, and used as a potting shed. It was obtained by Mersey Tramway Preservation Society members in 1983 and after restoration entered service on the Wirral Tramway in 1999.

Dudley single decker No 34, which was built in 1919, is now in regular use at the Black Country Living Museum.

Good as new: Wolverhampton open top tramcar No 49, which dates from 1909, was returned to traffic at the Black Country Living Museum in 2004 after a restoration lasting 25 years.

Birmingham Corporation Tramways double decker No 395 on display inside the city's Thinktank museum.

Right: The only surviving Bradford Corporation tramcar is No 104, preserved in Bradford Industrial Museum.

The Seaton Tramway gives birdwatchers unrivalled views of the River Axe estuary. Car 11, built in 2005 and based on design elements from Plymouth and Blackburn tramcars, heads towards Colyford.

Opposite: Seaton Tramway No 19, the sole surviving Exeter Tramways vehicle, built by Dick, Kerr in 1906 and now reduced and converted to a single-deck saloon. Exeter Tramways operated five routes between 1905 and 1931.

Car 10 departs Colyton, where the original London & South Western Railway village station building has been tastefully converted into a continental-style tram stop complete with tearoom and shop.

Right: Seaton Tramway open-top Car 12, a freelance design of 1966, prepares to depart Colyton.

Opposite: The new Seaton terminus built by the tramway in its 25th anniversary year sees 1968-built Car 8, an open topper based on a Llandudno & Colwyn Bay Tramway design, waiting with Nos 9 and 10, both of which were constructed in 2002.

Manx Electric Railway Car 5 and trailer at Baldrine Station. This 17-mile 3ft gauge electric inter-urban tramway links Douglas with Ramsey via Laxey, where passengers can change for the Snaefell Mountain Railway. Two of the original three cars that opened the line in 1893 are still in use, and are the oldest electric tramcars still at work on their original line anywhere in the world. Its trackbed is largely segregated from roadways. The line, very much a time capsule from the early days of electric trams, is run by the Manx government.

Opposite: The 3ft 6in gauge Great Orme Tramway in Llandudno is Britain's only remaining cable-operated street tramway and one of only three left in the world. It was built in 1902 to take passengers to the summit of the Great Orme headland and is in two independently-operated sections, each with two cars dating from the opening. Passengers have to change trams at the Halfway Station.

Manx Electric Railway-inspired toastrack tram at the Seaton Tramway.

Snaefell Mountain Railway tram No 5, seen high above the cloud line at the Summit Station. The five-mile 3ft 6in gauge line which runs up the Isle of Man's highest peak from Laxey opened on 20 August 1895 and still uses the original six tramcars, although No 5 had a new body built in 1970 after being all-but destroyed in a fire. It is electrified using overhead wires at 550V DC.

The Tramway Centre near Swansea Museum has the only surviving cab of a Swansea & Mumbles Railway tramcar, along with much memorabilia and a screened programme about the old railway. The centre is not open every day, so visitors should contact Swansea Museum on 01792 653763 first. Admission is free, as it is to Swansea Museum.

Glasgow Coronation tram No 1173 is preserved as part of the city's Museum of Transport collection. Glasgow Corporation ordered a fleet of 100 new double-deck trams, the first of which were delivered in 1937, the year of the coronation of King George VI. They were described as the finest short stage carriage vehicles in Europe.

Glasgow single decker No 1017, formerly Paisley No 17, was built in 1904 and now runs at Summerlee Heritage Park in Lanarkshire.

Belfast double decker No 357, was manufactured in 1930 and is now an exhibit inside the Ulster Folk & Transport Museum. The Belfast Corporation Tramways lines were electrified in 1905 and the last tram ran in 1954.

The Manchester Metro brought the street tram concept back into mainstream public transport in Britain. This is one of the first trams, the T-68 type, built in 1991-2 by the Italian manufacturer AnsaldoBreda.

Left: The volunteer-run 20in gauge Shipley Glen Cable Tramway is the oldest working cable tramway in Britain, apart from funicular lines. The quarter-mile line was opened on 18 May 1895, and was built to serve the local beauty of Shipley Glen near Saltaire in West Yorkshire.

Sheffield Supertram Car 104 at Gleadless Townend tram stop. Sheffield was the second UK city to open a new tramway in the 1990s.

Croydon found itself at the heart of experiments with new forms of tram in the late nineteenth century, and the location of the new modern Croydon Tramlink at the end of the twentieth. A Tramlink service is pictured heading for Elmers End.

Perhaps the most famous tram of all today is one that never was. In December 2010, to mark the 50th anniversary of the Granada TV soap opera, Coronation Street staged a Manchester Metro light rail tram crash which killed several regular characters. The mock-up tram body was subsequently donated to the city's Museum of Science and Industry. In 1989, Alan Bradley, a character in the series, died when he fell under the wheels of Blackpool tram No 710 outside the Strand Hotel on North Promenade.

Picture credits

Cover, 28 centre, 30,31,32,33,34,37,40,41,43 (all),44,45, 46 top,59,60,61 Paul Jarman, Beamish Museum; 2,55,57 Isle of Man Tourism; 5,58 Swansea Museum; 11,13,17, 20 (both) London Transport Museum; 22 Middleton Railway; 29 (both) Crich Tramway Village; 35 top Mark S Jobling; 36,37 Brian Lindop, Blackpool Tramways, 47,48 Black Country Living Museum; 50,51,52,53 Seaton Tramway; 54 Colin Paxton/Great Orme Tramway; 62 Tim Green/Creative commons; 63 Transport for London, 64 Granada TV.